# QUESTIONS: BELIEFS AND TEACHINGS

> 'I know; you believe; he is confused'
> (how bigots conjugate the verb 'to believe')
>
> 'With most men, unbelief in one thing springs from blind belief in another.'
> Georg Christoph Lichtenberg (1742–1799)
>
> 'Be not afraid of life. Believe that life is worth living, and your belief will help create the fact.'
> William James (1842–1910)
>
> 'We are born believing. A man bears beliefs, as a tree bears apples.'
> Ralph Waldo Emerson (1803–1882)

## People or beliefs?

Religious education's first concern is with children and young people: How are their views and opinions shaping up? What beliefs and commitments are they developing for life? Are they adding to the skills they need of disagreeing respectfully and articulating their own ideas clearly and deeply? In comparison to this central concern, the issue of what a particular religion teaches is merely a source for good learning in RE. The subject is for children to use the resources of faiths and beliefs to explore for themselves what it means to be human.

In this first book of a new series from RE Today, we offer four examples of compelling learning that teachers can use in the 11–16 age group which enable learners to explore some key beliefs and teachings from Muslim, Hindu, secular and Christian sources in ways that provoke their own thinking.

Lat Blaylock and Stephen Pett
Editors

## Key features

Here are five key features of this book and the RE Today series which it begins:

- **Being practical:** We provide practical, ready-to-use learning activities for RE teachers that are well thought out and set good standards for all learners. We include clear objectives, a wide range of learning approaches and accurate ideas about assessment.

- **Being adaptable:** We know that many good teachers like to adapt our materials for their own classes. While the materials are 'ready to use' in one form, they are also flexible and can be adapted in many ways to meet learning needs of different abilities and age groups, different syllabuses and qualifications. Adapt freely, and make the ideas better.

- **Being open to depth:** We prefer to offer well worked and properly developed ideas for study from a small number of religious sources rather than attempting to cover everything. In this book, three religions are used, alongside some secular material. The series as whole will enable learning from many more religions and beliefs, but depth always trumps mere coverage.

- **Being realistic:** The work we have developed for this series is the product of deep engagement with classrooms and pupils' needs, and is often trialled before publication. Our key question is: 'Will this work in the classroom?' We've failed if the answer is 'no'.

- **Being thoughtful:** We think that no good RE lessons happen unless pupils think for themselves, but this doesn't happen automatically. Thinking skills strategies are one way to achieve this, and we offer others too.

# WHAT IS BELIEF?
# WHAT IS RELIGIOUS BELIEF?

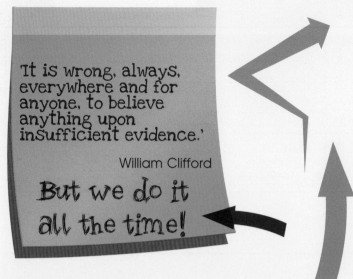

'It is wrong, always, everywhere and for anyone, to believe anything upon insufficient evidence.'

William Clifford

But we do it all the time!

## Can't be proved

Religious beliefs are unprovable convictions – or are they the choices we make about life, rationalised? The RE curriculum is often engaged with questions of belief, as this book is, but it isn't always easy to use the concept of belief clearly. This opening section of the book explores the place of the concept in RE. The QCA's English National Framework for RE, and new secondary curriculum for RE, uses the concepts of 'beliefs, teachings and sources' as a cluster. Scottish revised RME guidance talks of 'beliefs and values'. The implication is that religious beliefs at least are connected to the authorities, traditions and values of the faith. This is obvious at one level: Muslim beliefs are derived from the holy Qur'an and the life of the Prophet. Christians get their beliefs about God from Jesus, from their gospel records, understood through the traditional teaching of the church. However, when considering Hindu beliefs and atheist beliefs, a fault line in this idea can be detected.

## Different ideas

Hindu traditions, so diverse and complex, picture religion as the 'sanatan dharma', the eternal way. Your faith and your life are never separated, and the beliefs of Hindus are not summarised in any creeds or codified in universally – or even widely – accepted ways. Gandhi said the only belief Hindus share is that cows are sacred (but some Hindus disagree with that). Even if belief is a good way to understand Christianity or Islam, a different conceptual toolkit might be needed for learning from Hindus.

## Atheists: negative?

Among atheists, there is some reluctance to agree that atheism is a belief. If the sources of authority for atheists are human reason and argument, then being an atheist is not a belief, but a conclusion to an argument. This is awkward when intelligent theists pursue the dispute, because the ground on which the argument takes place seems to shift, to be different according to the person holding the floor. The debate about God, for example, which will not go away, remains the significant border at which humanists and atheists skirmish with Muslims and Christians.

## Honest broker? You?

Perhaps the RE teacher can be an honest broker with regard to questions of belief. One starting point is to distinguish belief from knowledge, from the provable, and to admit happily that belief in what is not proved is a feature of every human life. Some people are more credulous, inclined to trust what is believed. Others are more sceptical, rejecting received beliefs. All of us sometimes give more weight to a belief than the strict criteria of data, evidence and argument might allow. This could lead to classroom dialogue in which the words 'proved' and 'disproved' were banned, and only the language of evidence, probability and argument were permitted. A modest improvement in clarity might be achieved by this. Another clarifying thought is that for many people, the beliefs they hold are so tightly interwoven into their lives and values that the cerebral act of believing can never be separated from the whole process of living.

In this book, our writers have provided starting points for learning that will energise and even excite your pupils, as they enquire into the big questions: What are my beliefs? What impact do they have? Why can't I prove much about the big questions? Who has influenced me in the beliefs I hold? How are they changing? Why are beliefs so diverse? How can anyone get close to the truth when ideas are so varied? What kinds of test can we bring to beliefs that can't be proved? The next two pages make space for collecting some early ideas from your classes. Ask them to fill in the sheets and use the results for conversation and evidence in the following lessons.

RE Today Services

# The language of belief

Think about the spiritual beliefs you've studied in RE (including those of Christians and Muslims, Hindus and atheists perhaps). Give us a sentence for as many of these prompts as you can, and make it detailed, thoughtful, witty or controversial.

| | |
|---|---|
| I think . . . | |
| I doubt that . . . | |
| I am sceptical about the claims of . . . | |
| I think there is no good evidence for . . . | |
| I reckon there is strong evidence for . . . | |
| Maybe . . . | |
| Perhaps . . . | |
| My opinion is . . . | |
| Personally, I believe . . . | |
| I'm sure that . . . | |
| My conviction is . . . | |
| I would bet my life that it's true that . . . | |
| I'm convinced that . . . | |
| I'm committed to . . . | |
| You cannot prove . . . | |
| If you want to test . . . | |

One belief I really disagree with is . . .

My argument is . . .

A person who has influenced my beliefs is . . .

This person made a difference by . . .

One thing I used to believe, but don't now, is . . .

Because . . .

# Beliefs

One belief that matters to my parents, but not to me is . . .

A reason is...

'Everybody lives by beliefs. We can't be really certain of much.'

I think . . .

Two ways my beliefs make a difference to what I do are . . .

And . . .

My definition of a belief is . . .

What this means is . . .

RE Today
Services

# KARMA, PUJA, REFLECTION AND BELIEF

Exploring responses to Hindu ideas: a stimulus for personal reflection with 11–13s through an interview, a poem, a shrine exploration and a game

This section of *Questions: Beliefs and Teachings* provides starting points that will engage pupils with some key Hindu ideas and practices. Hindu traditions are so diverse that teachers should be cautious about over-generalising. Here we present some mainstream ideas found in British Hindu traditions, but the variety is endless. There are four pages to copy for the class (pp.8–11), and the activities, aims and attainments are described on the first three pages. An interview, a poem about the mystery of the divine, a simple game and a way of building understanding of worship are provided. Taken together, these activities can engage learners with teachings and with their own beliefs.

**Aims for this work** include enabling pupils to:

• develop their awareness of the significance and impact of religious beliefs on individuals

• understand the impact of some Hindu ideas and practice on ways of life

• reflect on and express more clearly their own ideas about meaning and purpose in life

• consider insightfully the challenging mysteries of varied beliefs about God or the divine.

## Activity 1
## Aum explored

'Aum' signifies the Hindu belief that God is all that there ever was, is and will be: the first sound of the universe, the beginning of meditation and the seed of all other mantras.

Pupils could:

• develop and compare a range of symbols for eternity of their own.

• research the many meanings of 'AUM', using some carefully selected websites.

• produce a PowerPoint presentation or poster that explains some of the multiple meanings of the symbol.

## Activity 2
## Using a poem to explore Hindu beliefs about God

The poem on p. 8, in 11 four-line stanzas, enables exploration of questions about the divine from Hindu and other perspectives through the questions it raises. A potentially profound starting point can use the musicality and rhythm of the language: get your pupils to read it aloud.

## Activity 3
## Using artwork or presentation to show understanding of key terminology

In groups pupils work together to produce posters that explain the meanings of diva, arti, bhajan and mandir.

a **Research** using carefully selected websites such as www.hindunet.org

b **Art work** such as a large diva, arti tray, Indian instruments, mandir outline or pictures of gods or goddesses, could be done using paint, collage work, tissue paper, glitter and fabric

c **Explanations** decided upon in groups and added to posters

Alternatively, after step (a) pupils could choose to prepare a presentation on each item, perhaps with performance too.

## Activity 4
## Making music

Pupils could compose their own hymn that praises creation or the creator; add a musical accompaniment, followed by performance.

## Activity 5
## A Hindu home shrine explored

**Design and make activity:** Ask students in groups to design a sensory reflection area/ home shrine suitable for a Hindu family. Steps for this may include:

- reading what Saksham and others say about their home shrine and its value and importance to them

- identifying what essential elements are needed – what things will they touch, taste, see, hear, taste? Identify and gather the materials, artefacts, textures, and make an appropriate setting.

### Designing my own shrine

Gather students around a shrine and read what Saksham said about his 'special place'. Allow a moment for their own quiet reflection. Students could then complete the following personal reflection: 'If you had a family shrine, what ideas of God would you have in there and why?' Remind pupils Hindu gods and goddesses are visual representations of the innumerable facets and talents that make up the one Ultimate, the universal principle, Brahman. Offer pupils the option of having symbols or objects rather than deities or people on their own 'shrine'. Also include the option for those of no belief in the divine to reflect on who or what do they or would they worship and why.

## Activity 6
## Moksha patuma (Snakes and Ladders)

**Exploring Hindu beliefs about karma (actions and consequences)**

Hindus believe that the soul passes through a cycle of successive lives (*samsara*) and its next incarnation is always dependent on how the previous lives were lived (*karma*). **Karma** means action, and law of karma is law of action and its consequences. Hindus say that we have to take responsibility for everything we do. Everything we do will produce results we have to bear. Sometimes the results of our actions are felt immediately, sometimes we see them much later. The law of karma teaches Hindus to be mindful in everything they do.

In the game, copiable from p.10:

- good deeds are represented by the ladders – which eventually lead to *moksha* (escape from the death and rebirth cycle (*samsara*)) – the ultimate goal.

- evil actions are represented by the snakes which lead back to the cycle of rebirth. Provide each group of four players with a board, a pack of 10 cards from p.9 and the game instructions.

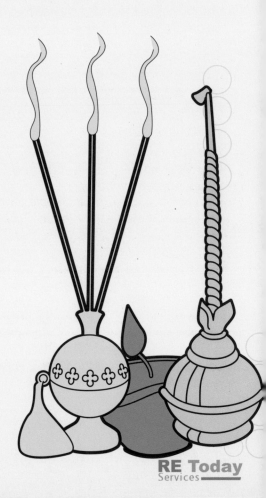

**RE Today**
Services

# Meet Saksham

Saksham is 11 years old and lives with his parents and brother Dhruv in Wrexham. He and his family are Hindu. We asked him four questions.

## What does worship mean to you?

'Worship to me means a way of getting closer to God. To wish for something you really want and to confess all your sins and crimes. It's something that makes my family feel close.'

## How does worship make you feel?

'It makes me feel very relaxed and very happy from the inside. I think it's a good way of communicating with and getting your feelings across to God and to other people. I usually worship with my family, but there isn't a Hindu community in Wrexham, only a few Hindu people. I have different feelings when I worship just with my family and when we are part of a large group worshipping together. I can be more open when I'm with my family but it's also great with more people as you feel part of a group and proud to be there.'

## Where for you is your most spiritual place?

'My most spiritual place is a **temple** because it's a special place of worship for Hindus. However, there isn't a Hindu temple in Wrexham, so living here means I also feel the **shrine** (place set aside for worship in our kitchen at home) is also a very spiritual place for me.

'Every evening at about seven, we all gather at the shrine to worship and pray as a family. There are big pictures of different gods and goddesses, such as **Durga** who is a goddess that sits on a tiger to show how powerful she is, and **Ganesh**, who has an elephant head and is believed to be very wise, which I like to look at. This is a peaceful and special time in the day.'

## If you could pick one object to represent worship for you, what would it be and why?

'My special symbol would be the **Aum** mainly because it's the symbol for the Hindu religion, so I feel it's my symbol. It also means a lot to me as **it represents God**. I worship God *as* the Aum symbol and *by using* the Aum symbol.'

# Who?

by Sri Aurobindo (1872–1950)

In the blue of the sky, in the green of the forest,
Whose is the hand that has painted the glow?
When the winds were asleep in the womb of the ether,
Who was it roused them and bade them to blow?

He is lost in the heart, in the cavern of Nature,
He is found in the brain where He builds up the thought:
In the pattern and bloom of the flowers He is woven,
In the luminous net of the stars He is caught.

In the strength of a man, in the beauty of woman,
In the laugh of a boy, in the blush of a girl;
The hand that sent Jupiter spinning through heaven,
Spends all its cunning to fashion a curl.

There are His works and His veils and His shadows;
But where is He then? by what name is He known?
Is He Brahma or Vishnu? a man or a woman?
Bodies or bodiless? twin or alone?

We have love for a boy who is dark and resplendent,
A woman is lord of us, naked and fierce.
We have seen Him a-muse* on the snow of the
mountains,
We have watched Him at work in the heart of the
spheres.

We will tell the whole world of His ways and His cunning;
He has rapture of torture and passion and pain;
He delights in our sorrow and drives us to weeping,
Then lures with His joy and His beauty again.

All music is only the sound of His laughter,
All beauty the smile of His passionate bliss;
Our lives are His heart-beats, our rapture the bridal
Of Radha and Krishna, our love is their kiss.

He is strength that is loud in the blare of the trumpets,
And He rides in the car and He strikes in the spears;
He slays without stint and is full of compassion;
He wars for the world and its ultimate years.

In the sweep of the worlds, in the surge of the ages,
Ineffable, mighty, majestic and pure,
Beyond the last pinnacle seized by the thinker
He is throned in His seats that for ever endure.

The Master of man and his infinite Lover,
He is close to our hearts, had we vision to see;
We are blind with our pride and the pomp of our
passions,
We are bound in our thoughts where we hold ourselves
free.

It is He in the sun who is ageless and deathless,
And into the midnight His shadow is thrown;
When darkness was blind and engulfed within darkness,
He was seated within it immense and alone.

*Meaning 'as a muse'.

From Sri Aurobindo Society website:
www.sriaurobindosociety.org.in, used by permission.

## Using a poem to explore Hindu beliefs about God

- Begin by having two excellent readers prepare to read this aloud in the classroom. It is powerful!

- Ask pupils in threes to look at 1–3 verses each. What does the writer believe about God / the Ultimate?

- Put the verses of the poem on 11 separate cards. Ask students to organise them into what they think is the right order.

- Use 'directed activity related to texts' strategies: highlight the values/metaphors/adjectives/questions/descriptions of God in the poem.

- There are over 20 descriptions of God in the poem. Which ones would a Christian/Hindu/Muslim agree about? What would a Humanist say to them?

- Many of the lines of the poem are paradoxical and surprising. Which three are hardest to decode, to make sense of? What might they mean?

- Compare this to a creed, and to some Spirited Poetry 'God' poems (www.natre.org.uk ). How is it similar and how different?

RE Today
Services

## Moksha patuma (Snakes and Ladders)

The well-known game of Snakes and Ladders originated in India. It was originally a board game used by religious leaders to teach children about the difference between good and evil – climbing up the ladders representing good, and sliding down the snakes representing evil. The law of karma in Hinduism is a law of action and consequences: what you give out is what you get back. If you do something good you are rewarded – if you do evil you will reap the consequences. Here are examples of good ways of living: do they stand for the ladders in the game? What would the snakes symbolise?

| **Non-violence** | **Truthfulness** | **Non-stealing** |
|---|---|---|
| **(Ahimsa)** | **(Satya)** | **(Asteya)** |
| To respect all life as sacred. To practise non-violence in thought, word and deed, not only to people but also to animals, plants and the world of nature. | To always speak the truth, even if it does not make you popular. To do so in a friendly and agreeable manner. | To take nothing for yourself which has not been given or gained as the result of your own efforts. |
| **Compassion** | **Steadfastness** | **Honesty** |
| **(Daya)** | **(Dhriti)** | **(Arjava)** |
| To be kind to people, animals, plants and the Earth itself. To practise forgiveness. To sympathise with those who are suffering and in need – the poor, the elderly, the sick. To oppose abuse and cruelty. | To work to achieve your goals with prayer, purpose, persistence and push. To develop willpower, courage and industriousness. To refuse to let opposition or fear of failure change your determination. | To do what is right even in difficult times. To reject deception and wrongdoing. To avoid cheating or deception. To face and accept your faults without blaming others. |
| **Moderate appetite** | **Purity** | **Divine conduct** |
| **(Mitahara)** | **(Saucha)** | **(Brahmacharya)** |
| To avoid over-eating, and to avoid meat, fish, shellfish, fowl or eggs. To follow a simple diet avoiding rich and fancy foods. | To practise purity and cleanliness in body, mind and speech. To maintain a clean and healthy body. To avoid harsh, angry or bad language. | To be celibate whilst single and faithful when married. To dress modestly, shun pornography, sexual humour and violence. |
| **Patience** | | |
| **(kshama)** | | |
| To restrain intolerance. To be calm and agreeable. To remain composed in good times and bad. | | |

**Applying the learning:**

- When pupils have played the game then the learning discussion can explore the meanings of karma and moksha. Does each square stand for a separate life? The road to moksha is long. Can good deeds enable better futures? Who believes this?
- Ask pupils in pairs to devise another board or card game that expresses the sense of life as a journey, and to prepare to play this new game with a group in the next lesson.

# Moksha Patuma:

a game of chance, triumph and disaster (just like real life)

## Instructions for playing the game

You need: Four players; a playing board; a single die (dice) and dice-shaker; coloured counters/buttons for playing pieces, and a set of concept cards (p.9). It is a good idea to be clear about the rules before the start of the game.

### Rules for playing

- To begin: all players roll the dice and the player with the highest score goes first and rolls the dice again to move. The race to the end of the board begins.
- In turn each player rolls the dice and moves his playing piece along the squares in accordance with the number rolled. More than one playing piece can occupy the same square. There is no extra turn for rolling a six.
- When a player lands on a square containing the foot of a ladder, she moves up the ladder, takes a card from the pack, reads it out and suggests a practical way this Hindu principle might be put into action in life today. For example when picking up the Ahimsa card the player suggests a practical illustration of non-violent action. If she has given a good response (in the view of the other players) they move on one additional square from the top of the ladder.

- When a player lands on a square containing a snake's head, he moves down the snake to the end.
- The winner is the first player to attain moksha by reaching the end of the board: square 100. The exact number needs to be rolled on the dice, either by remaining on a square of 94 or above, and waiting until the required number is rolled, or by moving to 100 then reversing back, according to the number rolled on the dice. Decide at the beginning of the game which rule to follow.

**Afterwards: In what ways is this game like life, according to Hindu ideas and according to your own ideas?**

**Make a list.**

© Sophie Hardwicke

**Worshipping at home:** Match up the items in the drawing with the descriptions, and explain the meanings of each after you have read the description below. Why is home worship important in Hindu life, do you think?

© Clare Jarvis

# Objects found on a home shrine

Many different objects are found on a home shrine include pictures of the gods and goddesses, and sometimes a picture of a deceased loved one.

**The items used in puja might often include:**

- A small lamp (usually a dish with a cotton wool wick placed in vegetable oil or clarified butter)
- A small bell
- Freshly picked flowers and leaves
- Freshly drawn water in an iron or copper vessel
- Incense burning in a holder
- Red kum-kum powder or turmeric powder or sandlewood paste, for making the Tilak mark on the worshipper's forehead
- Food offering of sweetmeats and fresh fruit.

# WHY SHOULD I LEAD A GOOD LIFE WHEN 'THE GOOD LIFE' IS ON OFFER?

## Summary of learning

It is not always easy for young people to understand why the holy scriptures of the world religions have such authority in believers' lives. There are various reasons why students might reject such authority; this unit looks to get them to examine the message of the Bible (and therefore its authority for believers) in the light of the impact of belief on people's happiness.

This series of lessons examines the messages behind a source of authority in many students' lives – advertising, which values and promotes The Good Life. Students then compare these messages with some of the ethical injunctions of the Bible – encouraging people to live 'a good life'. In order to get students to evaluate these two approaches to life, it then explores some of the findings of psychologists as to what makes people happy. Who is more likely to be happy – someone leading The Good Life, or someone seeking to lead a good life?

## Connections

In this work, learning can connect:

- students' own ideas with ideas from secular worldviews and Christianity
- RE and psychology – exploring what makes human beings happy
- RE and media studies or English – analysing the messages of TV and print advertisements
- units on Christianity, or the message and authority of the Bible
- cross-curricular dimension – critical thinking.

## Useful websites

www.tellyads.co.uk

www.bestadsontv.com

This unit encourages critical evaluation of the varied messages that bombard students every day, as well as giving them pause to consider the wisdom of some ancient teachings. Such open-mindeness and critical awareness is central to good RE. The impact of beliefs on people's lives is at the heart of secondary RE – and the lessons that can be learned for students' own happiness and wellbeing make 'learning from RE' an integral part of the process.

LE MAQUILLAGE

Surely you're worth it

Come on! Dive in! Live the good life!
Refreshing – invigorating – fizzing – rejuvenating!
Be beautiful!    Be alluring!

## Questions

- What are the values behind advertisements?
- What do they suggest is most important in life?
- How different is the message of the Bible?
- Whose messages should we trust?
- Is it bad to want 'The Good Life'?
- What makes you happy?
- Can you do anything about it?
- Some prefer to think of bliss later rather than pleasure now. How about you?

RE Today
Services

## Activity 1
## Examining The Good Life

a Watch a selection of adverts from www.tellyads.com

- In pairs, decide what they are trying to say about what matters most in life. What gives life meaning and purpose? What values do they express?
- Write your ideas in the spaces provided on the right.

b In groups, make lists of at least five effects on individuals, families and society if these values were central to their lives.

c As a class, come up with a description of society if we could all live The Good Life.

### Extension

Some people would argue that these adverts promote a secular, materialist way of life – one with no reference to religion or a spiritual dimension. Look at this quotation from a Muslim journalist:

*Enlightened Muslims . . . must continue to . . . remind (secular materialists) of the **distressed, atomised and utterly lonely society** which they have created through aggressive individualism, where the habits of obligation and duty have been obliterated.*

Yasmin Alibhai-Brown

d In pairs, reflect on how far she is right. How good is The Good Life? What 'habits of obligation and duty' have been obliterated? Are there other benefits that compensate for this, do you think?

e Write a short letter of 250–300 words to Yasmin Alibhai-Brown expressing your view and giving reasons for your conclusions.

A Powerpoint to support this activity is available to subscribers on the RE Today website www.retoday.org.uk

e.g. freedom to roam; freedom from limitations; control

## Activity 2
## What is a good life?

**a** Have a look at these quotations. In pairs, decide what they are trying to say about what matters most in life. What gives life meaning and purpose? What values do they express?

| | | |
|---|---|---|
| A man will leave his parents and be united with his wife, and the two will become one flesh. What God has joined together, don't let human beings separate. | Be on your guard against all kinds of greed; a person's life does not consist in how much stuff they have. | The person who loves their life will lose it. The person who gives up their life to serve God in this world will keep it for eternal life. |
| When you give, don't do it in public for everyone to see - people who do that have already had their reward. | Let your 'Yes' mean 'Yes' and your 'No' mean 'No'. Don't pile up empty words. | The fruit of the Holy Spirit is love, joy, peace, patience, kindness, goodness, gentleness, faithfulness and self-control. |
| Don't worry about tomorrow - tomorrow will take care of itself. | Feed the hungry, care for the homeless, be kind to the desperate. That's what religion really means. | Human beings look at the outside appearance, but God sees what really matters - your heart! |
| You'll be happy if you are hungry and thirsty for justice. One day it will be yours! | Be thankful whatever happens. | Love your enemies - do good to those who hate you. |
| Love your neighbour as much as you love yourself. | Do not lord it over people. Whoever wants to be great must be like a servant. | Love God with all your heart and with all your soul and with all your strength. |
| If I can know the future and if I give my money to the poor, that's all useless if I don't have love. | Do not be overwhelmed by evil. Instead, overwhelm evil with goodness. | Live your life like this: do what is just. Love what is merciful. Walk with God. Don't be proud. |

**b** In groups, make lists of at least five effects on individuals, families and society if these values were central to their lives.

**c** As a class, come up with a description of society if we could all live a good life, according to these statements.

**RE Today** Services

## Activity 3
## Who is happier?

Look at the values you have identified as representing The Good Life in advertisements, and a good life as seen in the Bible. Write 200–250 words explaining which set of values would lead to happiness. Which makes you happier – The Good Life or a good life? Explain why you think this.

## Activity 4
## Who is happier? Going deeper

Bearing in mind your response to Activity 3, look at the table below. Work out whether A or B is happier. Mark an X on the line to show your answer. Explain why.

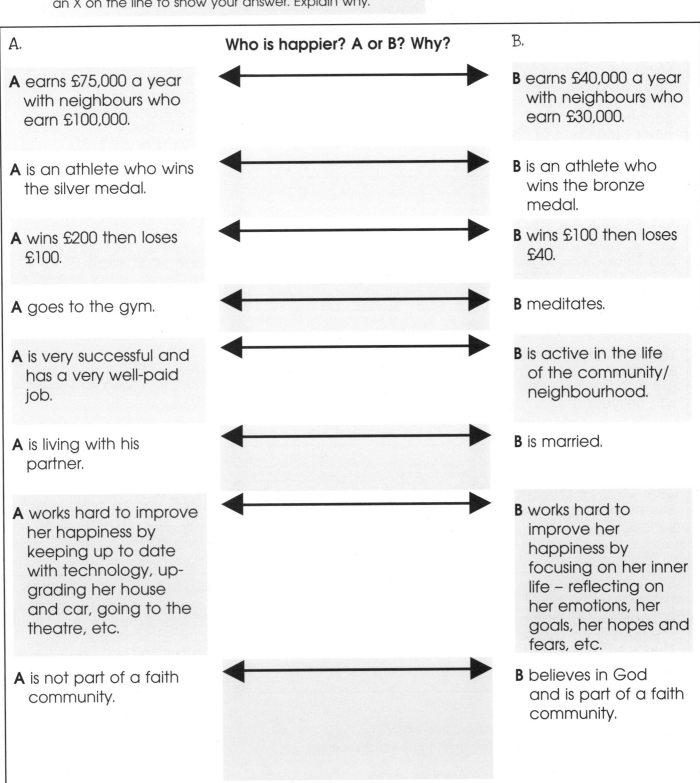

A.

Who is happier? A or B? Why?

B.

A earns £75,000 a year with neighbours who earn £100,000.

B earns £40,000 a year with neighbours who earn £30,000.

A is an athlete who wins the silver medal.

B is an athlete who wins the bronze medal.

A wins £200 then loses £100.

B wins £100 then loses £40.

A goes to the gym.

B meditates.

A is very successful and has a very well-paid job.

B is active in the life of the community/ neighbourhood.

A is living with his partner.

B is married.

A works hard to improve her happiness by keeping up to date with technology, up-grading her house and car, going to the theatre, etc.

B works hard to improve her happiness by focusing on her inner life – reflecting on her emotions, her goals, her hopes and fears, etc.

A is not part of a faith community.

B believes in God and is part of a faith community.

## Activity 4
## The answers – what psychology tells us

Psychologists tell us that B is happier every time.

1 & 2 – we are happier if we can compare downwards than if we compare ourselves upwards. The silver medal winner compares herself to the gold medal winner; the bronze looks to the person who came 4th. Money doesn't seem to buy happiness. Once you earn more than about £14,000 a year, earning more money makes almost no difference to happiness.

3. Bad things have more of an impact on us than good things.

4 & 7 – working on self-understanding and balance has more effect than external circumstances.

5. High levels of trust are significant for happiness – which often links to active involvement in the local community.

6. Marriage is consistently one of the most important single factors in life satisfaction – mainly due to the sense of security and commitment derived.

8. 'One of the most robust findings of happiness research (is) that people who believe in God are happier' (Richard Layard, *Happiness: Lessons from a New Science* p.72).

**Important note:**

This material is not included to try and persuade students to become religious – that is not what we are about as RE teachers! It is here to encourage some genuine interaction with the values expressed in the adverts and in the Bible quotations. Is The Good Life really so good?

Of course, in terms of the psychology research, the question remains, are these people happier **because** of these commitments and beliefs, or do they hold them **because** they are more positive, happy people in the first place. . .? The truth or falsity of the beliefs are beside the point – but having **faith** seems to make a difference.

## Activity 5
## Drawing things together

Select from the following tasks to enable students to meet the expectations on p.18. All might start with tasks (a) and (b).

**a  Why should I lead a good life when The Good Life is on offer?**

Answer this question, referring to secular materialist ideas (as presented in the adverts) and Christian beliefs, as well as your own view.

- The adverts put across the idea that the most important values in life are. . .
- Individuals might find these (e.g. helpful/ unhelpful appealing/worthwhile/superficial, etc) because. . .
- If society lived by these values it would be . . .
- The Bible verses show that the most important values in life are . . .
- These are important to Christians because. . .
- Some of them, such as . . . might also appeal to people without religious belief because. . .
- The findings of psychology suggest that people with the biblical values (which might match those of people of many faiths) are happier, in general, than those who follow the values of the adverts. I think that this is because. . .
- I can see the value of living 'a good life' because. . .
- I can see the value in living 'The Good Life' because. . .
- I prefer to lead a good life/The Good Life because. . .

**b  Find or devise an advertisement for living a good life.**

What is the appeal of a good life? How might this inspire someone to live differently?

You might like your example of a good life to come from a religion or from a non-religious viewpoint. Humanist values may be used as an alternative to religious values.

**c  Write the script for a discussion between Jesus and the Chief Executive Officer (CEO) of one of the companies in the adverts.**

Why did Jesus give these instructions to his followers? What do you think motivated him? What motivates the advertisers?

What would Jesus be critical of? How would a CEO respond? How do the adverts reflect Western culture? What impact do the values expressed by the adverts have on society?

**d  Write a guide for Christian living in the twenty-first century.**

Why is The Good Life more seductive than a good life? Why is it hard to be a religious believer in today's world? How do you handle the consumerist message?

RE Today
Services

| What does Lionel Shriver think The Good Life is like? | To be almost ridiculously sweeping: baby boomers and their offspring have shifted emphasis from the communal to the individual, from the future to the present, from virtue to personal satisfaction. Increasingly secular, we pledge allegiance to lower-case gods of our private devising. We are less concerned with leading a good life than The Good Life. We are less likely than our predecessors to ask ourselves whether we serve a greater social purpose; we are more likely to ask if we are happy. We shun values such as self-sacrifice and duty as the pitfalls of suckers. We give little thought to the perpetuation of lineage, culture or nation; we take our heritage for granted. We are ahistorical. We measure the value of our lives within the brackets of our own births and deaths, and don't especially care what happens once we're dead. As we age – oh, so reluctantly! – we are apt to look back on our pasts and ask not 'Did I serve family, God and country?' but 'Did I ever get to Cuba, or run a marathon? Did I take up landscape painting? Was I fat?' We will assess the success of our lives in accordance not with whether they were righteous, but with whether they were interesting and fun. | How far do you identify with Shriver's Good Life? Knowing what you now know about the psychology of happiness, how happy do you think she is? Why? | **Jesus began to teach:** |
|---|---|---|---|

To what extent is this a fair picture of it or a caricature? (Shriver was brought up in a committed Protestant Christian family.)

Lionel Shriver 2005

http://www.guardian.co.uk/books/2005/sep/17/society

**Jesus began to teach:**

How happy are the humble-minded, for the kingdom of Heaven is theirs!

How happy are those who know what sorrow means, for they will be given courage and comfort!

How happy are those who claim nothing, for the whole earth will belong to them!

Happy are those who are hungry and thirsty for goodness, for they will be fully satisfied!

Happy are the merciful, for they will have mercy shown to them!

Happy are the utterly sincere, for they will see God!

Happy are those who make peace, for they will be known as children of God!

Happy are those who have suffered persecution for the cause of goodness, for the kingdom of Heaven is theirs!

*The Bible*, Matthew 5: 3–10 (J B Phillips translation)

## Jesus' 'Beatitudes' – his formula for happiness

1  What would Lionel Shriver's 'Beatitudes' look like? Compare them with Jesus'.

2  What is the significance in the cultural differences between Jesus' life as a poor peasant in first-century Israel, and Lionel Shriver's life as a wealthy American author and journalist living in twenty-first century UK? (Level 7 task)

3  Write down how the following people might respond to Shriver's creed and Jesus' 'Beatitudes':

   a  A nurse in the UK
   b  An atheist engineer working in a refugee camp in Sudan
   c  Nelson Mandela
   d  An AIDS orphan in Africa
   e  A political prisoner in China
   f  You

4  Write your own 'Beatitudes'. Show that you have learned from this unit about the benefits of The Good Life and a good life.

## Outcomes

This unit challenges students to think carefully about the assumptions often made about the value and desirability of Western consumerism, and the irrelevance of biblical teachings.

The best students will be able to discern what is of value from both perspectives, whilst showing a critical awareness of their own viewpoint.

Ideally, students will have some idea of the costs and benefits of living 'The Good Life' and living 'a good life', to themselves and to others.

Pupils can demonstrate achievement at levels 5–7 in these activities if they can say 'yes' to some of these 'I can . . .' statements:

### Level 5  I can . . .

• **explain how adverts express** a non-religious approach to life, and how the Bible expresses a religious approach to life. **I can compare the two and say how they affect** the lives of individuals and communities.

• *express views on the difficulties of being a Christian and following Jesus' teachings in a society full of these non-religious adverts, and relate this to my own life.*

### Level 6  I can . . .

• **give an informed account** of how Christian beliefs about meaning and purpose differ from a secular view as shown in adverts. I can explain why these values differ and explain the differing impact they may have on the lives of individuals and communities.

• *express my own insights on why some religious people are unhappy with the world as it is, and explain my own response to this.*

### Level 7  I can . . .

• **show a coherent understanding** of the ways in which religious faith may help people be happier, and how they address questions of meaning and purpose.

• *evaluate the significance of Christian and non religious responses to questions of meaning and purpose in comparison with my own.*

## Resources

1 This unit works best with clips of TV advertisements.  Thousands are available from www.tellyads.com.  If the technology is not available, it would work with print adverts. Select some from a range of magazines. Ask students to bring in adverts for things that they have subsequently bought. Then you can find out what effect the advert had on them. They can still analyse the print ads to identify what values they present as being most important.

2 Have a look at the article by Martyn Percy in *REtoday*, Autumn 2008, for inspiration about how adverts may be used in RE.

3 Richard Layard's book *Happiness: Lessons from a New Science* (Penguin, London 2006) is a useful introduction to ways in which research into happiness may have an impact on policy and education.

4 For a brief account of happiness studies from a Christian perspective, read 'Life Coaching and Well-being' by Bruce Stanley, which appeared in *Bible in TransMission*, Winter 2006. The activity on p.15 draws upon this work, with the permission of the Bible Society. http://www.biblesociety.org.uk/l3.php?id=311

5 Yasmin Alibhai-Brown's comment comes from her article in the *SHAP Journal* 2002/2003 ('Don't tell me how I should worship').
This site is a rich resource for RE teachers (www.shapworkingparty.org.uk).

### And if you've done all that . . .

You might like to look at Dylan Bartlett's excellent Farmington Fellowship paper on teaching happiness in RE. See the Farmington website:

www.farmington.ac.uk.

# CONTROVERSY, CREEDS AND CREDULITY

Enquiring into Muslim and Christian beliefs

## Summary of learning

Controversy is the lifeblood of RE in some ways. A good RE lesson often includes a good argument. The subject is about truth claims in uncertain fields of enquiry. This sequence of activities for good RE is all about getting 14–16 year old students to explore their beliefs and the beliefs of Muslims and Christians, with controversy as a tool for the enquiry.

Using two interviews, a writing frame and some statements of belief or creeds, learners get the chance to clarify and give reasons for different beliefs. They spend time enquiring into agreements and disagreements between Christian and Muslim believers. The work finishes by asking pupils to create a creed or an anti-creed of their own.

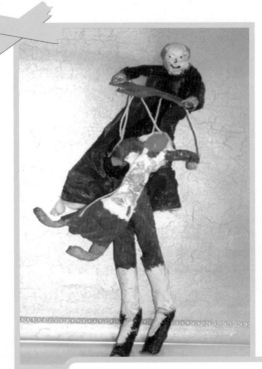

**Puppet on a string?** Do Christians believe that God is like your puppet master? Why does Islam teach that Allah rules over all? Should we love God, submit to Allah? Why? What do you believe about human freedom?

## Connections

In this work, learning can connect with:

- Pupils' own ideas and ideas from Christianity and Islam
- Syllabus units on beliefs, teachings and sources
- Philosophy and psychology of religion, including the methods of 'Philosophy for Children'.

### Useful websites

- 65,000 people have shared their childish beliefs on the website 'I used to believe . . .' The site is at http://www.iusedtobelieve.com. Better for the teacher to go and choose a few examples to introduce the lesson, as there are some fruity examples of beliefs about sex.
- A good gateway for Islam is www.islamicity. com. Teachers can use the section on the Five Pillars for introducing Muslim belief and practice.
- A good place to explore the impact of Christian belief is at www.rejesus.co.uk/lives. Your pupils can explore the impact of Christian beliefs on the famous from C S Lewis to Mother Teresa.

### Examinations

In the GCSE and Standard Grade examinations, pupils study reasons for belief about God. This work connects to all these syllabuses.

### Community Cohesion

This work also connects to RE's Community Cohesion priorities, especially where the exploration of diversity focuses on how to handle the fact that we all believe different things. The questions of what tolerant and respectful disagreement look like are at the heart of RE.

### Questions

- What do you make of Christian and Muslim statements of belief?
- What has influenced the beliefs you hold?
- How are our beliefs expressed, in words, in life and in art?
- What difference does belief make?
- What impact do your beliefs have?

# Task/action/thinking/questions

On the following pages you will find the resources you need for these activities.

## Activity 1
## A journalist's task to open an enquiry into religious belief

a Give each student a copy of p. 21, and ask them to work in pairs. Students interview their partners and record their points of view. Encourage them to do this in depth and with as much detail, argument, justification and explanation as possible. Make sure your interviewee uses as many as possible of the concepts and ideas in the box. Ask plenty of supplementary questions to dig out his or her ideas. Give a sweet (just one) to the best: it's amazing what they will do for one little sweet.

b Change partners, and everyone who has been interviewing becomes an interviewee. This generates 30 filled-in sheets about the significance of religious belief.

c If possible, send all the class to do another interview with an adult out of school for homework. They should choose someone they know who has interesting ideas about religion and belief. This adds another 30 samples to the data the students can work with.

## Activity 2
## Reader's research

Copy pp. 22 and 23 for students to use, again working in pairs. Each of them must read either Razwan's page, or Trevor's page. The two interviews on these pages use the same questions that students have been working with themselves. When pupils have had time to read the interviews, they are to identify four things that Razwan and Trevor agree on, and four things they disagree about. Students can record their responses to this thinking on a copy of p. 24.

## Activity 3
## Varied creeds: disagree to learn

Use these three creeds. Ask pupils to explain the reasons for the lines in these creeds with which they most disagree.

## A Humanist creed

I believe there is one life, and one opportunity to live it.

I believe in the reality and value of this world and everything in it.

I believe in separating truth and reason from superstitions and myths.

So I'm committed to this life, the environment and to science.

I believe that every human being can make the world a better place.

I believe that unselfish choices make peace and love.

I believe that love, laughter, pleasure and imagination give meaning to human life.

So I'm committed to human rights, the golden rule and living life to the full.

## Allah: Muslim belief

He in his essence is one, without any partner
Single without any similar
Eternal without any opposite
Separate without any like
He is one
Prior with nothing before him
From eternity without any beginning
Abiding in existence without any after him
To eternity without an end
Subsisting without ending
Abiding without termination
Measure does not bind him
Boundaries do not contain him.

   Al Ghazali, medieval Muslim theologian

## A modern Christian creed

We believe in God who was before all things and from the love of whom we cannot be separated.

We believe in his Son, Jesus Christ, who is one together with the Father and with the Holy Spirit who came down from heaven and became flesh for our sake.

He took human form. He humbled himself for our sake and suffered the degradation of torture and crucifixion.

God raised him from the dead to his glory and to life everlasting. We live in expectation of this glory.

We believe in one universal church and for the cleansing of sins through baptism. We look for the coming of God's kingdom.
Amen.

RE Today
Services

# A framework for writing a personal and critical evaluation of someone else's beliefs

Your interviewee's name:

Vocabulary and concepts: How many of these can you use in completing this questionnaire?
BELIEVE/CONVINCED/PROOF/ EVIDENCE/ CERTAINTY/DOUBT/ HYPOCRITE/ COMMITMENT/FAITH/ DEBATE/ARGUMENT

What is a religious belief?

Why do religious beliefs matter?

What do you think is the difference between opinions, beliefs, convictions, and feeling certain?

What belief is most important to you? Who and what has influenced you in holding this belief?

What should teachers of RE remember when they teach about beliefs?

We asked him to tell us about beliefs from his point of view.

## What is a religious belief?

Religious belief is a conviction. It is having a deep faith in something you cannot see with your eyes. It is a framework of reference by which one judges and perceives the world.

## Why do religious beliefs matter?

Religious beliefs matter because we are composed of matter (body) and spirit (soul). If the body is hardwired to want to eat, sleep, work and play, then your soul is inwardly seeking the ultimate truth. Religious belief fills the vacuum of the soul. Religious beliefs are like the currency of the soul. They give your heart prosperity. We rarely stop to think that 'BELIEF' has such an impact on our day-to-day life. 'Money' only works because we BELIEVE it has value: the actual piece of printed paper is pretty worthless. Studies show that a placebo in medicine can often be as effective as a drug: why? Because of BELIEF. Religions provide detailed, coherent information to help to order one's life in an otherwise chaotic world.

## What do you think is the difference between opinions, beliefs, convictions, and feeling certain?

In Islam there are three levels of certainty (yaqin) which come from the Qur'an:

## Ilm al-Yaqin – knowledge of certainty

Example: You are told that there is a fire in the forest. You research and see smoke coming from the forest. This is information and leads to knowledge.

## Ayn al-Yaqin – source of certainty

Example: You investigate further by going into the forest and you see the fire burning. This is confirmation and your conviction is made stronger.

## Haq al-Yaqin – truth of certainty

Example: Your face is illuminated by the fire/you become one with the fire. This is the truth of certainty and the ultimate reality. The universal quest is to find God and discover him through the three stages:

1 Knowledge through books
2 Sourcing deeper knowledge through contemplation and reflection
3 Finding truth through union

An opinion may or may not be correct. For example: have I got the right concept of God? Is there life after death? There is an old Sufi saying: 'You are either subjective in your objectivity or objective in your subjectivity.' This isn't a circular argument, it expresses the fact that lots of truths can simultaneously co-exist. With God, all things are possible. The Qur'an teaches that Christians and Jews and anyone who believes in God and works righteousness will taste Heaven and Allah's pleasure.

I distinguish between something that is 'more Real' and something 'less Real' by looking deeply into my soul and the Qur'an. If the intellect, soul, spirit, and the Revelation are in union then for me that is the ultimate certainty.

## What belief is most important to you? What has influenced you in holding this belief?

I believe that there is a universal deity who is the source of everything. He is a being without imperfection. He brought us into existence and we know him through his creation, his revelations and his effects on our souls. The Holy Qur'an, the sayings of Prophet Muhammad and the works of Muslim scholars, scientists and Sufi mystics, and also meditation and scientific reflection, have helped shape my belief in the universal divine being, which in Arabic is Allah. I praise him and thank him for bringing me this realisation.

## What should teachers of RE remember when they teach about beliefs?

RE teachers should always bear in mind that sometimes beliefs can be very powerful and positive. Many wonderful buildings of the world have been created through religious belief. Science owes a lot of its history to religious people, as do music and art. Religious conviction has inspired humankind to soar beyond the material, to transcend base matter, towards union with a higher soul, from conflict to union, peace and realisation.

**RE Today** Services

# Dr Trevor Cooling is a religious educator and a Christian

**We asked him to tell us about beliefs from his point of view.**

## What is a religious belief?

A religious belief is an articulation of what one thinks is the case concerning some aspect of reality. For example: 'Jesus is the Son of God'. It's a belief because, even though beliefs usually are (and in my opinion should be) supported by reason and evidence, they are always an interpretation of the evidence and can therefore be contested by others who have come to a different conclusion. A *religious* belief, to me, is one that says something about the significance and meaning of human life. That means that Humanism would be classified as religious believing. That's not a problem for me, although I know Humanists don't like being classified as religious so I am also happy to distinguish between religious and non-religious beliefs and use 'worldview' as the all-encompassing term instead of 'religious'.

## Why do religious beliefs matter?

Because they shape the people we are and become. If we believe, for example, that every person is created in the image of God, then we will (or at least should) treat them differently than if we believe that life is nothing more than the evolutionary struggle for survival. And yes, they claim to describe reality. If it really is true that life after death is a reality, that does matter a bit! I think it's important to spend a little serious thinking time on that – in between the partying, of course.

## Would you distinguish between opinions, beliefs and convictions? How and why?

Most definitely. Opinions have a 'take it or leave it' character. I think that Cheltenham is the best place in England to live: so what? – that's just my opinion. But beliefs, well they are different. As a Christian I believe there will be a new creation some time in the future that will involve everyone. That's of a bit more consequence than just an opinion. Many beliefs are therefore held as convictions. I would argue that religious beliefs are held with what is called universal intent: we think they apply for everyone, not just us. In other words we think they are true. Actually I would say, I *know* when talking about my beliefs. I know Jesus is the Son of God. But I do absolutely recognise that that is contestable.

Most human knowledge is pretty subjective in that most of the really important things in life require interpretation: for example, whether to marry this person. I am pretty sceptical about the idea of objective certainty, things that people can't disagree on. Most of them seem pretty trivial to me. What matters in life is what some people call personal knowledge, which I suppose is another way of saying beliefs.

## Can you give an example of belief which you hold dear? What has influenced you in forming and holding this belief?

That creation is a work of God. My first degree is in biology. To be honest I cannot make sense of the world that I discovered in my biology without the concept of a designer God. So I am committed to what is called the anthropic principle: the belief that the fact that everything is just right for life to exists points to a Creator. I know that Richard Dawkins will mock this and tell me design is only apparent. That's his right, his belief, his interpretation. But I go with another top-flight geneticist Francis Collins who believes in a creator God. As I said before, beliefs are by their very nature contestable because they are *interpretations* of the facts.

## What should teachers of RE remember when they teach about beliefs?

Beliefs are really important and always contestable. Students need to be responsible for the beliefs they hold, because they are so important in shaping their attitudes and behaviour. It's the RE teacher's job to ensure students take this responsibility seriously. Forming their beliefs could be the most important thing they do in their education. But they also need to be aware that their beliefs, however convinced they are of them and however passionate they are in their commitment to them, are always contestable. Part of living in a diverse society is learning to relate to other people in a way that takes this tension between our commitment to and the contestability of religious beliefs seriously.

# Enquiring into Muslim and Christian beliefs

| Razwan, a Muslim, believes . . . | Trevor, a Christian, believes . . . | They agree that . . . | They disagree about . . . . | I think . . . . |
| --- | --- | --- | --- | --- |
| | | | | |
| | | | | |
| | | | | |
| | | | | |

RE Today
Services

## Outcomes

Many pupils will, through this work, achieve a clearer sense of their own beliefs and a deeper understanding of the beliefs of others.

Another significant outcome is the development of attitudes of respect. This is part of RE's contribution to enabling pupils to develop attitudes that connect to Community Cohesion and respect for all.

Another area where evidence of achievement can be seen is in relation to Citizenship. The work enables pupils to engage with diversity of belief, from Christian, Muslim and their own perspectives.

Tackling Tough Questions

## Resources

1  Teachers will find much stimulus to consider questions of belief in *Tackling Tough Questions*, Professor Russell Stannard's 85-minute DVD programme about questions of evil, suffering and death, viewed from many different perspectives. Published by RE Today.

2  The BBC's new series of '40 Faiths', adapted for schools from Peter Owen Jones' *Around the World in 80 Faiths*, is available at www.bbc.co.uk/learningzone/clips. A riveting resource!

3  From RE Today, more active learning and thoughtful RE is available in the following related publications, all available from www.retoday.org.uk or on 0121 472 4242:

- Engaging with RE: *Thoughtful RE*
- Engaging with RE: *Philosophical RE*
- Developing Secondary RE: *Questions about God*
- Developing Secondary RE: *Science and Religion.*

Pupils can demonstrate achievement at levels 5–7 in these activities if they can say 'yes' to some of these 'I can . . .' statements:

### Level 5  I can . . .

- explain the differences and similarities between two different sets of religious beliefs.
- express my own views about the meaning and importance of religious beliefs, using religious and philosophical terminology well.

### Level 6  I can . . .

- interpret the similarities between Muslim and Christian creeds, and the ways they differ from Humanist beliefs for myself.
- express insights of my own into the diverse beliefs and views I've studied.

### Level 7  I can . . .

- use the methods of philosophy to give coherent accounts of different understandings of religious belief.
- draw balanced conclusions of my own about key issues in religion and belief.

### And if you've done all that...

The British Library has a fine website section drawn from its 'Sacred' exhibition. The section on beliefs can be found at: http://www.bl.uk/onlinegallery/features/sacred/wfabelief.html

# BIOGRAPHY OF BELIEF

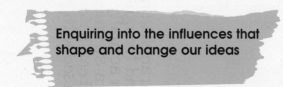

**Enquiring into the influences that shape and change our ideas**

## What to do: five activities

1 **In the right order** Copy the next two pages onto card (preferably two different colours) and cut up some sets, one between three for the class. Begin by asking groups of three pupils to put the cards they have in a biographical order. Several different ways of doing this are possible, none is right. Discuss this with the groups.

2 **Compare two 'biographies of belief'** Next get a trio who have worked on the Muslim example to join up with a trio who have done the atheist example, and compare notes. Ask them especially to list five similarities between the two 'biographies of belief' and five differences.

3 **Why do beliefs keep changing?** Third, run a whole class discussion about the ways in which belief changes, and especially is subject to influences. Ask the class to identify examples of experiences, people and arguments that are influential in our two biographies – and on them too.

4 **What might happen next to Dawud and Richard?** Ask the trios to produce three more statements to add to the biography they studied, suggesting where the 'biography of belief' might go next. They can write further diary entries for the atheist and the Muslim as if they were 30, 50 or 70 years of age, for instance.

5 **Create your own 'biography of belief'** Finally, ask the students to think through their own biography of belief, and write at least six moments when key experiences, arguments and people have influenced their beliefs, to deepen or to challenge their ideas.

Beliefs change as we live. Experience makes a difference to what we think. Sometimes religion is pictured as fixed and unchanging, but most people find their beliefs varying as time passes. This learning activity uses some card-sorting activities to set up a piece of writing by pupils about the ways their own beliefs have changed, and may be changing. It will work well for pupils in the 13–15 age range. Examples are provided here using Islam and atheism.

There is an extension activity for high-achieving pupils that introduces the perspectives of psychology of religion and philosophy of religion. One part of the learning intentions in the work is to enable students to see some links between philosophy of religion and psychology of religion.

Pupils can demonstrate achievement at levels 5–7 in these activities if they can say 'yes' to some of these 'I can . . .' statements:

### Level 5  I can . . .

- express views about the ways beliefs are shaped and changed for both an atheist and a Muslim.
- explain clearly some influences on my own beliefs.

### Level 6  I can . . .

- use religious and philosophical concepts coherently to explain beliefs and influences upon them.
- give informed accounts of influences upon beliefs and the impact of beliefs, including my own beliefs.

### Level 7  I can . . .

- use different disciplines (e.g. psychology of religion, philosophy of religion) to carry out an independent critical enquiry into beliefs.
- use sources, evidence, arguments and examples to develop critical analysis of religious, philosophical and spiritual questions about beliefs.

I feel like I'm drifting away from God and religion at the moment. I've been a bit lazy with my prayers, I guess, but in honest truth, I've hardly missed it at all. Perhaps I'm growing out of religion. Maybe in a year I won't even be a believer! Scary thought – Some people will be very annoyed if that happens!

An amazing thing today, I didn't think I'd bother going to the mosque for Friday Prayer, but I'm so glad I did. It was packed, and I felt a real connection to everyone, a real spiritual high from being there. Felt really near to Allah. Not sure why, but good, and very interesting.

It's six months since Gran died now. After all my doubts and thoughts of atheism, I feel I am actually a stronger Muslim and a stronger believer than I've ever been before. I hope she would be pleased with me.

My parents are strong Muslims. I really admire the way they take their religion seriously, but they also respect other people and their different beliefs. I am questioning my own beliefs, and telling them I might be an agnostic. They tell me I will grow out of it, and I should do my prayers more often.

This was the first year I completely kept Ramadan. I did the fast properly from sunrise to sunset every day, and I didn't cheat. This has really helped me to have more faith and to deepen my commitment to being a good Muslim. I didn't even find it hard to give my zakat!

Today there was another stupid story in the press about Muslims and terrorists. I am sick of how my religion is shown on telly. You'd think we were all bombers, but Islam means peace. Sometimes I wish I wasn't a Muslim, but it's not really a choice. I do believe in Allah.

My gran is teaching me to pray every day at the moment. I always like it: first I watch her, then she gives me her attention. She is always calm when she prays, but at other times she is a bit of a shouter. I like her best at prayer times, and this is helping me to trust God.

When Gran died, last month, it was really sudden, and devastating. I cried and I prayed. Some people find death drives them away from God, but for me, I felt Allah was really guiding me and giving me comfort. I'll never forget my gran. She was a good woman.

At school today, in RE, there was big argument about atheists and believers. Lots of the others are atheists, but I thought I'd better tell them why I believe in Allah. Then I thought: 'Why do I?' All I could think of was that I've been brought up to believe, which doesn't sound very convincing.

I went to a wedding last week, in a hotel. Nothing religious about it. I watched my cousin making her promises to her bloke, and I realised how hard it is to make a marriage work, but how important. I thought 'God help you!' Literally, I wanted them to get the help of a god. I kind of wished at that moment that I did have faith in God!

I've been doing some work at school on two charities that work for international development, Christian Aid and Islamic Relief. They're both very impressive, and it makes me think that there is more good done in the name of religion than I've noticed before. Faith: not all bad.

I've been through some interesting discussions lately about being an atheist or a god-believer. I think when I'm older, I will always be an atheist, but I do understand why some people trust God. I think I can't absolutely prove it either way until I die, anyway. Then I won't even know!

My grandad died this week. I'm only 13: I feel too young to cope. He has always been there for me, and I'm so shocked by his death. I feel sure he can't just have 'stopped being'. He was such a vital, real person. I feel sure he had gone somewhere, not stopped being. I just know it. This is not a religious thing for me, more like a philosophical idea.

Over summer I read a brilliant book by Bertrand Russell, the philosopher, called *Why I am not a Christian*. All my ideas about God, afterlife and souls make sense again, and I'm pretty sure of being an atheist again, after going through a time of questioning.

I've decided I want to be open minded. I was asking my dad about life after death, and he just laughed at me really, and it made me think he is a bit of a bigot. He never has new thoughts. Don't want to be like that.

My family have never been religious in any way. As a little kid I never went to church, and never sang a hymn. I never said a prayer when I was small. I suppose you could say I was indoctrinated to be an atheist. God was a swear word in our house, and religion has always been a joke.

My first friend at my new school has got me thinking about my beliefs. He is a Christian: he seems happy with his faith, intelligent and good fun – not what I expected. He's got me wondering if religion is as daft as I've been taught.

I've not suffered much in my life. But my auntie is in a wheelchair with her arthritis. I stayed at her house last week. She told me she can only cope with daily pain by trusting God. I thought: 'in that much pain, you'd never believe in God'. But she says faith really helps her.

RE Today
Services

# Philosophy of religion, psychology of religion: aiming high

## What enables high achievement for 14-year-olds?

Adding the use of some of the main methods by which religion is studied to your RE with higher-achieving pupils is a key way to set higher standards in RE. This reflects the English QCA's description of achievement for Levels 7 and 8 of the RE scale of achievement. It is best to introduce pupils to using methods from psychology of religion and philosophy of religion in very structured ways. In the activity below on p. 24, the methods of philosophers and psychologists are simply stated, and pupils are invited to use the biographies of belief from Dawud and Richard above to find examples that connect.

In groups of 4, give pupils a copy of p. 30, and discuss any difficulties they have with it. Ask them to think about the meanings of the three points made to introduce psychology of religion and philosophy of religion. Then ask them to write a paragraph each: What would the philosopher, the psychologist say about Dawud's beliefs, about Richard's beliefs? Get them to compare notes with another group of four, and combine their work to make the best possible commentaries on the 'biographies of belief' they have been studying. Collect the work to enable pupils to share their best with each other. Draw conclusions: Are the methods of psychology and philosophy helpful in exploring beliefs? What can we learn from these methods?

**Sian is 14. This piece of her artwork expresses her understanding of questions of belief. She writes about her work:**

### Where is God?

*To be honest, nobody really knows. Everyone has their own perceptions and opinions on who God is. My picture is the art form of a humble, open mind attempting to find the answer to this question Where is God? Naturally, our way of finding an answer is to ask more questions, seeking a deeper meaning or understanding. I have drawn a phone to symbolise the questions: 'Can I ring you?', 'What is your number?' The eye and hand symbolise other questions. The person whose mind this is wants to find God and wants to be guided through life. Sometimes religion is a way of finding emotional support and self-belief.*

# Psychology of religion: What does it mean? What does it do?

**1**

### Psychology explores family influences

- Psychologists explain how our families have influenced us, for good or for bad, for example how we sometimes accept and sometimes reject our parents' beliefs
- One question psychologists ask – and answer – is 'What experiences in your family life have led you think these thoughts?'

**2**

### Psychology looks at how people respond to big experiences

- Psychologists pay attention to how people react to big experiences like love, loss, rebellion, passion, explaining our responses to these events
- How do people behave when they are faced with suffering, rejection or death, or faced with pleasure, love and the power of life? Why?

**3**

### Psychology looks below the surface at motives and desires that may be hidden

- Some psychological methods disregard the surface of our lives and explore whether there is a deep, unadmitted desire or passion that explains our views or behaviour
- One example of this is that a psychology of religion may find insights into your ideas about God from your relations with your parents: do you see God as 'mother' or 'father'? Does that make you fear God, or love God?

# Philosophy of religion: What does it mean? What does it do?

**A**

### Philosophers clarify terms and concepts

- One method philosophy uses a lot is to look as words, concepts and ideas carefully, to make sure we know what we mean by them.
- So philosophers often ask: 'What does that mean exactly?' 'Can you explain that word more clearly?'

**B**

### Philosophers try to make arguments that work, and to kick out arguments that are not logical or valid

- An argument works if the conclusions are confirmed or even proved from the starting points.
- Philosophers of religion ask: What can be proved? What does the evidence show? What can we be sure of here?'

**C**

### Philosophers are interested in how we search for the truth, how we get to be certain or to know

- When a claim is made, philosophers test the evidence. Does the argument support the claim? What counts as evidence or proof?
- When someone claims to be sure (e.g. an atheist, or a theist) philosophy asks: How do you know this? What evidence do you have? What would count as proof or disproof?

**RE Today** Services

# ACCESS

The four examples of ways to work with beliefs in this book are all flexible to meet the learning needs of lower-achieving pupils. Here are four ideas to enable the reader to make the work simple.

**1   Modified writing frames:** Use simplified outlines for gathering pupils' ideas on p.3, so that pupils practise the same skill several times. Using six of the simpler prompts twice each, and leaving out the higher-order language skills of some of the others gives practice to pupils who need it. You might use:

- Maybe . . .
- Perhaps . . .
- I think . . .
- My opinion is . . .
- I'm sure that . . .
- Personally, I believe . . .

Ask pupils to work on these with a partner, or with a teaching assistant in a small group. Emphasise the need to 'think for yourself!' Similar adaptions can be made to the copiable outlines on pp. 4, 17, 21 and 24.

**We have placed a PDF of these adapted sheets on the website for members (password inside the *REtoday* back cover each term).**  **W**

**2   Multi sensory group work on a Hindu shrine:** Activity 5, on p. 6, asks pupils to create a model of a Hindu home shrine, based on the drawing on p. 11. This activity is specially suited to a 'learning by making' approach. Why not give this opportunity to a small group of pupils with these skills? Ask them to talk to others in the class about how they make it, and spend two lessons creating a model from which others can learn. Encourage them to see what beliefs lie beneath the surface of each object as they work.

The objective of getting pupils to respond sensitively to aspects of Hindu worship (Level 2 in RE) can be observed in action, rather than in a written task or test.

Pupils might like to take photos of their shrine as they create it, and make a presentation of 'how we did it' to the class. This covers the skills of self-management and team working (PLTS).

**3   Adverts for the good life!** The learning activities about advertising and the goals and purposes of life on pp.12–18 ask for higher-level responses from most pupils. Your lower-achieving children can be asked to watch the adverts, and decide on three feelings words that the product is supposed to give the buyer. Keeping this simple is useful for other pupils too: share the 'three words' and see if everyone agrees. Talk to the class about the way that adverts often try to sell you a drink, car or shampoo by associating the thing you buy with some feelings you like.

To give lower-achieving pupils a simpler task, you might ask them to create an advert for a religion: what are the 'selling points' of Islam, or Christianity?

**4   My biography in nine lines.** The 'biography of belief' learning activities on pp. 26–30 ask for extended writing from pupils, and the use of methods from philosophy and psychology of religion. To make this work more accessible, ask pupils to create a 'nine line biography'. This consists of nine sentences that tell their life story, and nine comments that all begin 'at this point I believed . . .' Reusing this simple prompt enables pupils to access two big ideas central to the work: Beliefs change over time. They are influenced by experiences and relationships.

A writing frame may help to 'scaffold' this learning approach. The emphasis should be on linking up experiences and beliefs in a simple way. Level 3 asks for pupils to make links between experiences and beliefs.

# CHALLENGE

High-achieving pupils in RE deserve to have their needs met, and their abilities, gifts or talents developed. This page suggests four ways to adapt the work in the book to inspire your most able pupils.

## 1   Analyse the language of belief.

The writing frames created around the class from the templates on pp. 3 and 4 provide rich data for analysis. When your high-achieving pupils have got their own sheets done, get them to analyse the work of others (from their own, or a different class) and answer these two questions:

- Do other learners' sheets show that the language of belief is used carefully, or carelessly? Give examples from both sides.
- What kinds of reasons for the beliefs we hold do people give? What is a 'good reason'? Give some examples.

This enables pupils to collaborate to deepen their understanding of the focal point of the work: how we use the language of belief. The skill of separating well-thought-out from less well-thought-out involves some discriminating thinking.

## 2   Who is God?

The poem by Sri Aurobindo on p. 8 of the book is the deepest piece of writing we have used in this resource. Ask pupils who are particularly talented with words to compare it with another poem or hymn about God. It is interesting to use a statement of the atheist position, or a hymn about God from a non-Hindu tradition. Ask pairs of gifted pupils to prepare a performance of the two texts they have studied, and an analysis: What do the two agree about? What questions do they leave unanswered? What do they disagree about?

This comparison approach works best if the skills of evaluation are 'wrapped up' in a judgement task, so get your pupils to say which text is the best poetry, the best philosophy, the best to read aloud. And ask them which one they agree with most too. Using poetry alongside prose provides another interesting point of comparison.

## 3   'Faith makes you happy': Test the evidence.

The work on adverts on pp. 12–18 includes the intention that pupils should be able to give a coherent account of why religion may make people happier than money or consumerism (Level 7). Ask your most able pupils to jump straight to this task, and create their accounts, using evidence from their own research. Then they compare these accounts with each other, and test out who found the best evidence and who used it in the best ways. The skill of separating evidence from arguments is a good one to draw to their attention.

## 4   Razwan, Trevor and someone else

Pages 22 and 23 give responses to interview questions from a Muslim and a Christian. Independent learning skills matter in good RE, so ask your most able pupils to go and interview some more people with interesting beliefs, to the same format. There are questions to use in the texts, but the students may think more deeply if they have to generate questions of their own. A digital voice recorder is an asset here – borrow one if you don't have one in the RE department. Students can edit the replies into text: our two examples are just over 600 words each. That should be enough!

RE Today Services